Fourth Position Shifting Exercises

for the Cello

by Cassia Harvey

CHP228

©2013 by C. Harvey Publications All Rights Reserved.

6403 N. 6th Street

Philadelphia, PA 19126

www.charveypublications.com

Fourth Position Shifting Exercises for the Cello

1

Cassia Harvey

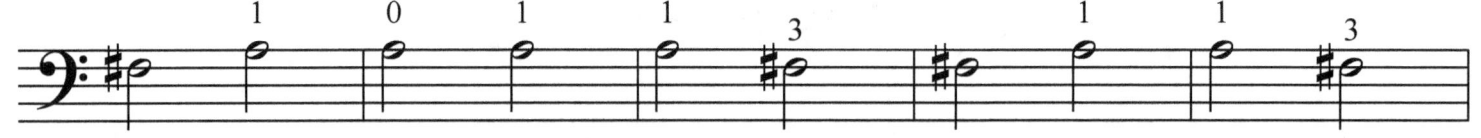
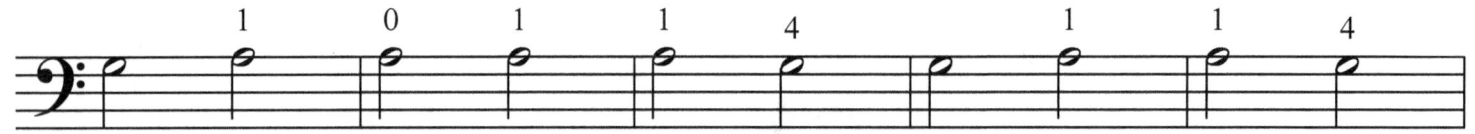
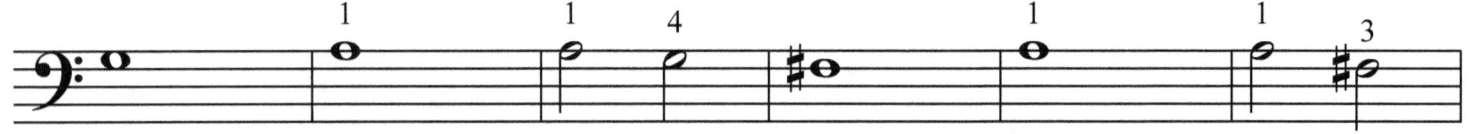

Fourth Position Shifting Exercises for the Cello

2

Fourth Position Shifting Exercises for the Cello

3

Fourth Position Shifting Exercises for the Cello

4

5

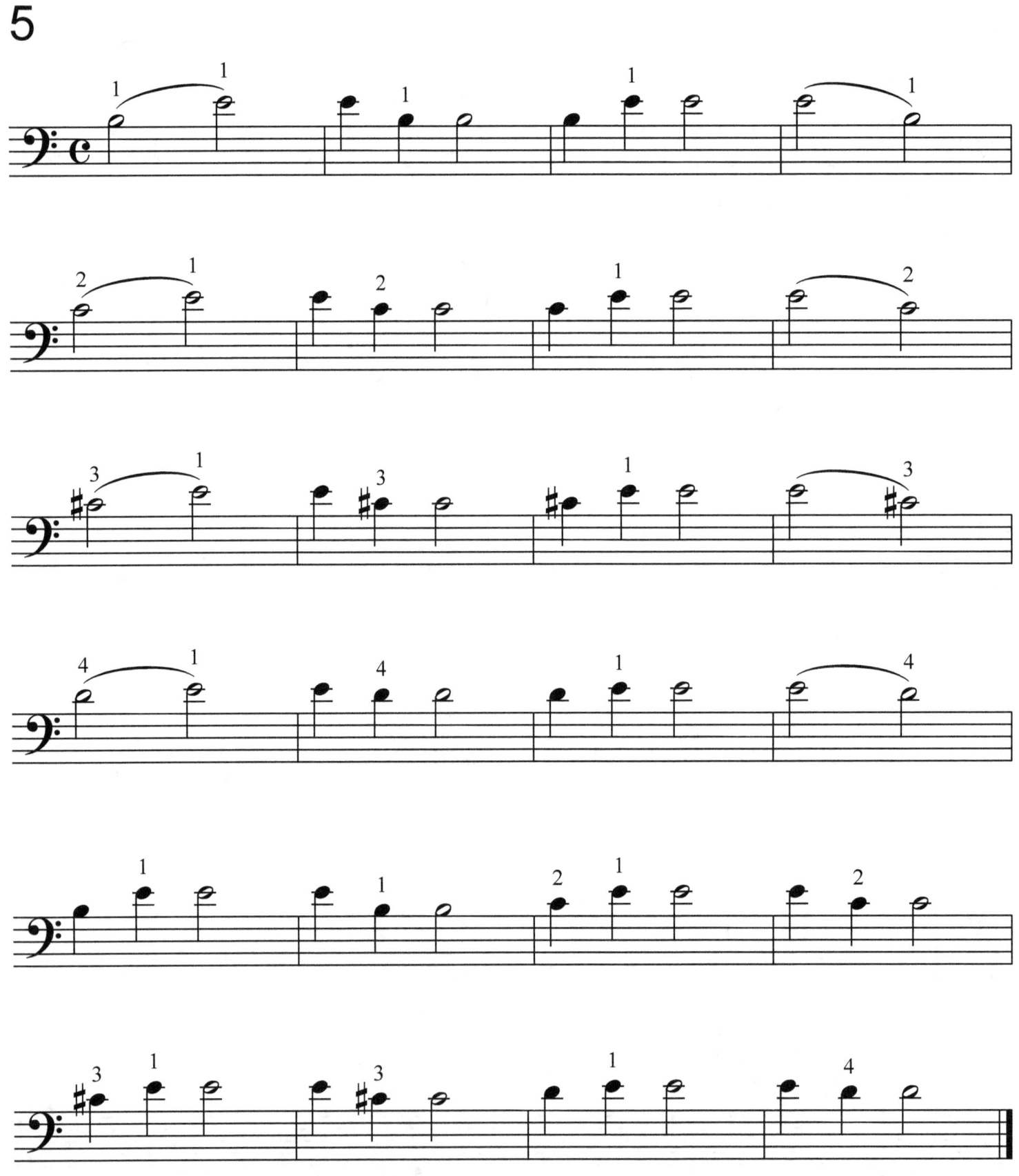

Fourth Position Shifting Exercises for the Cello

6

CHP228 ©2013 C. Harvey Publications All Rights Reserved. www.charveypublications.com

7

Fourth Position Shifting Exercises for the Cello

8

Fourth Position Shifting Exercises for the Cello

10

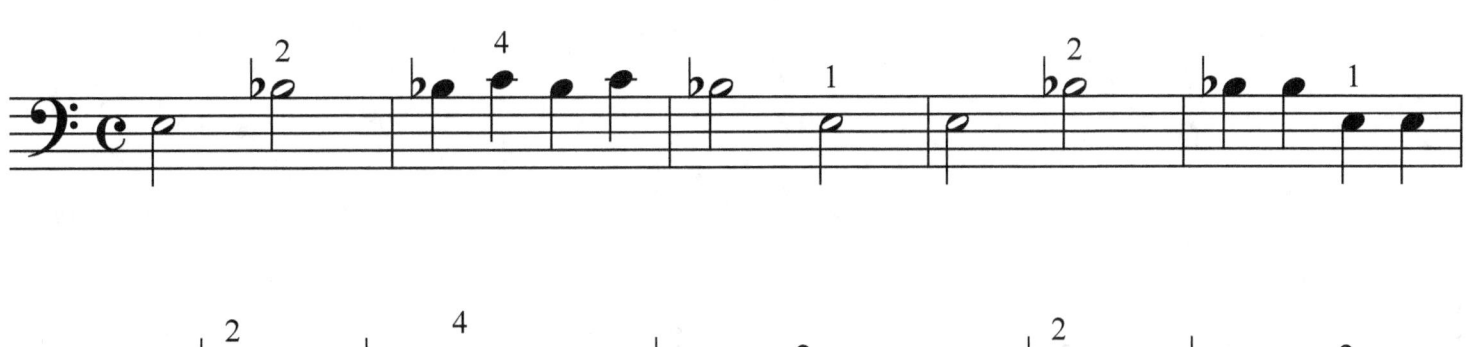

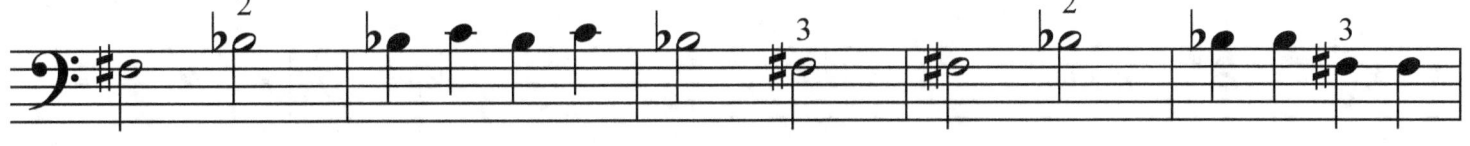

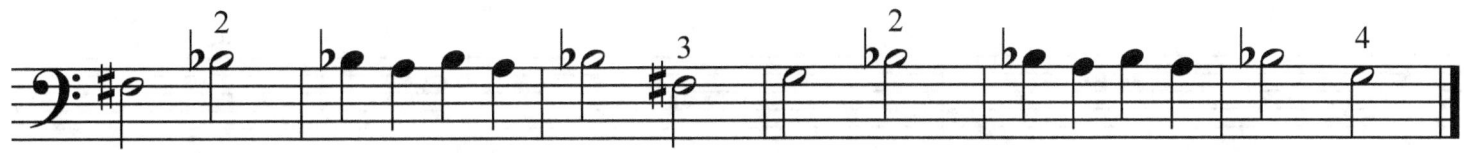

11

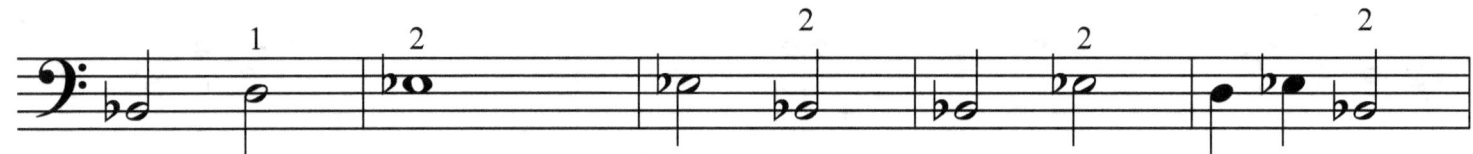

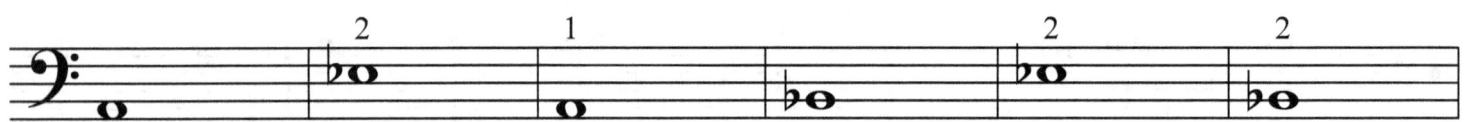

Fourth Position Shifting Exercises for the Cello

12

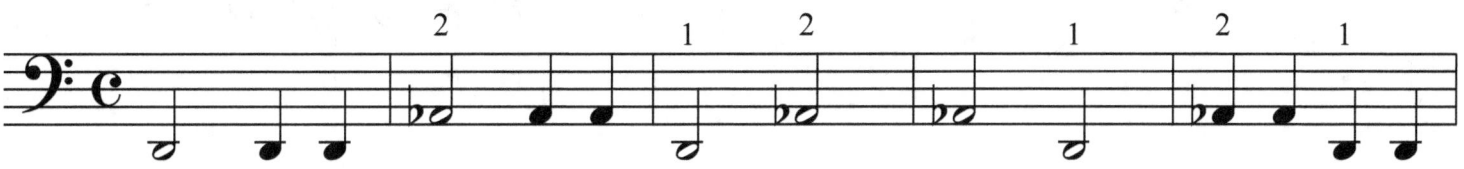

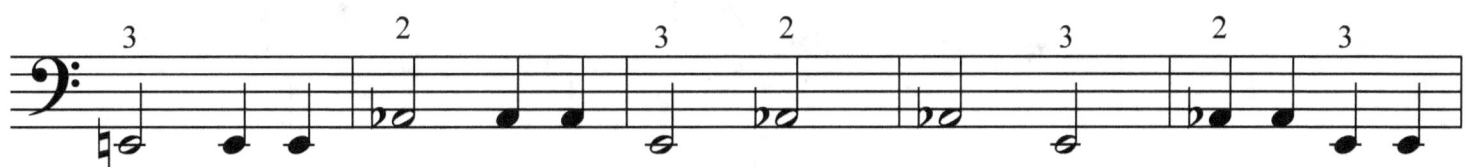

13

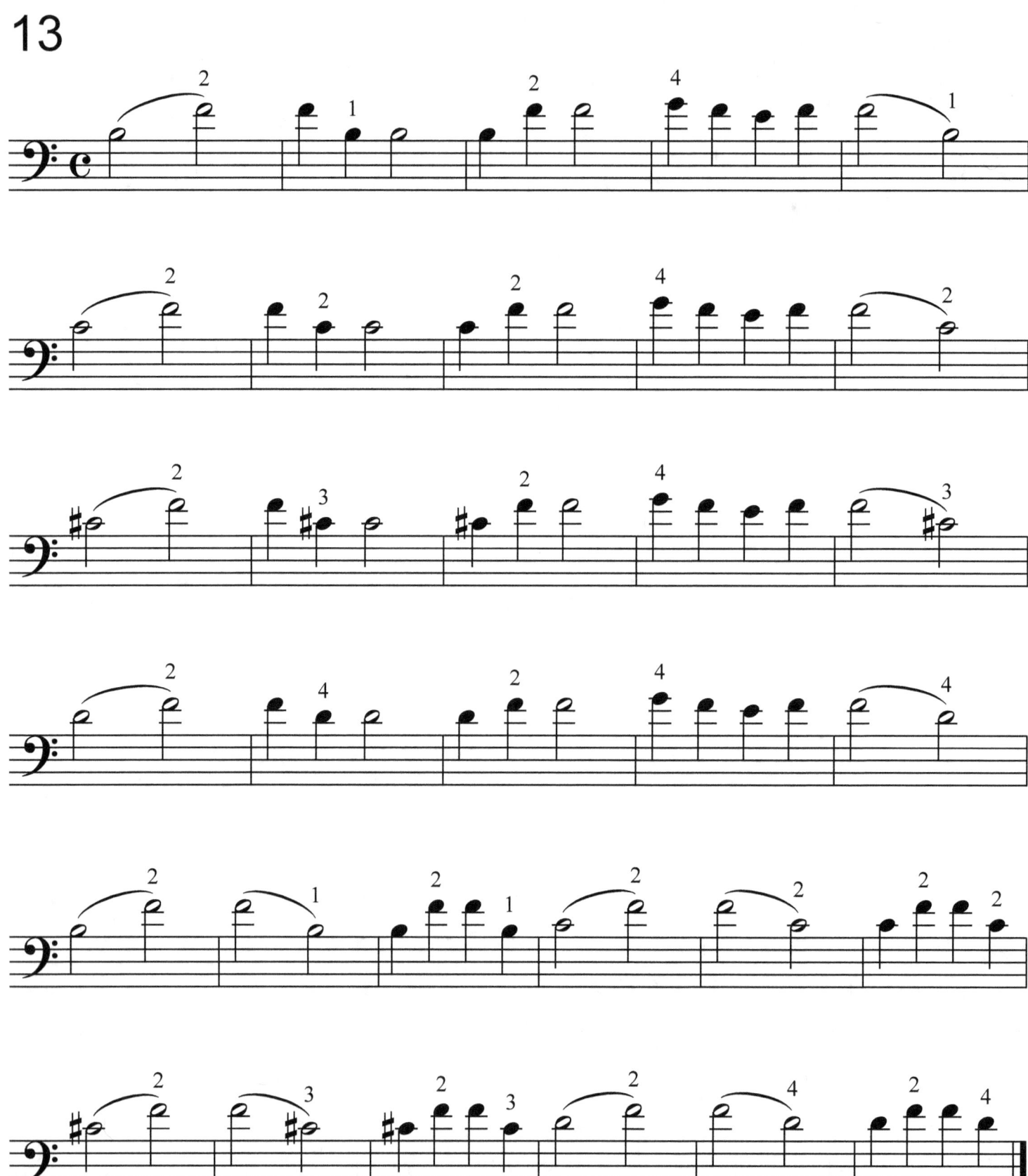

Fourth Position Shifting Exercises for the Cello

14

15

Fourth Position Shifting Exercises for the Cello

16

17

Fourth Position Shifting Exercises for the Cello

18

Fourth Position Shifting Exercises for the Cello

19

Fourth Position Shifting Exercises for the Cello

20

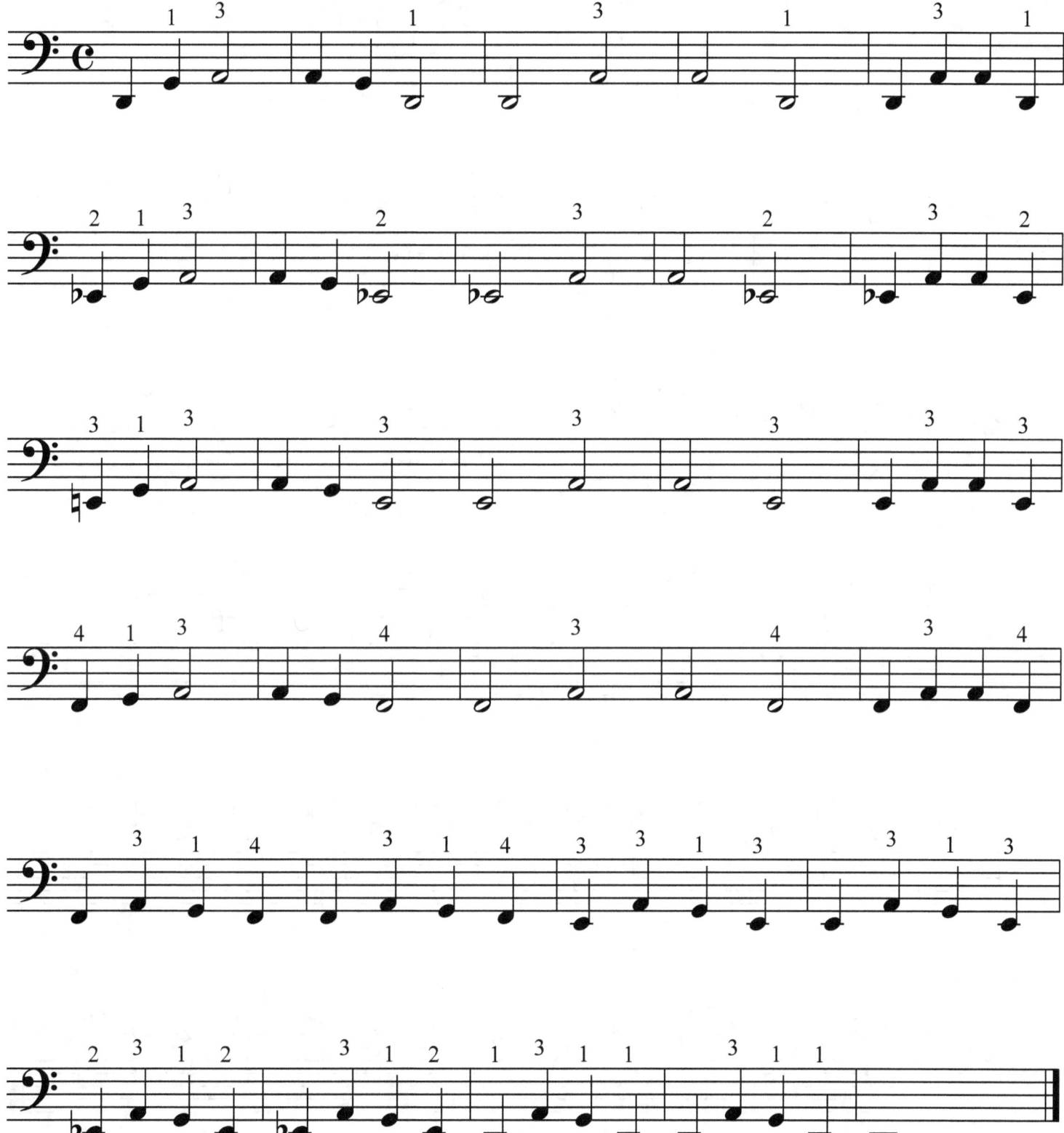

21

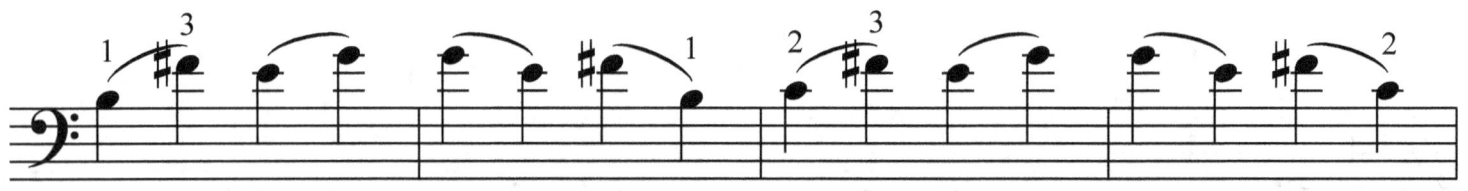

Fourth Position Shifting Exercises for the Cello

22

23

Fourth Position Shifting Exercises for the Cello

24

25

Fourth Position Shifting Exercises for the Cello

26

27

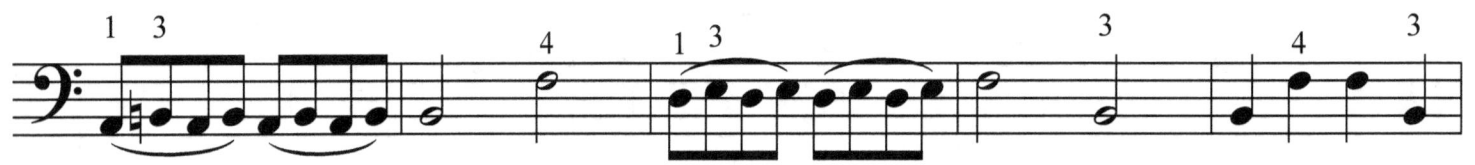
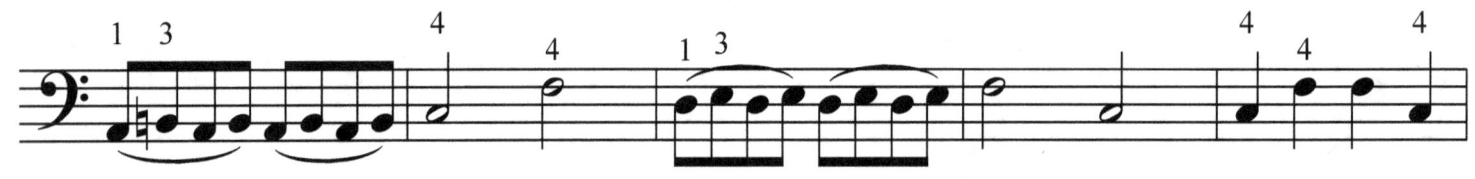

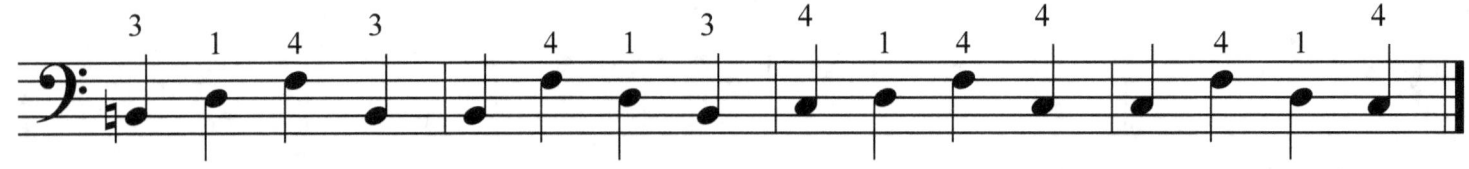

Fourth Position Shifting Exercises for the Cello

28

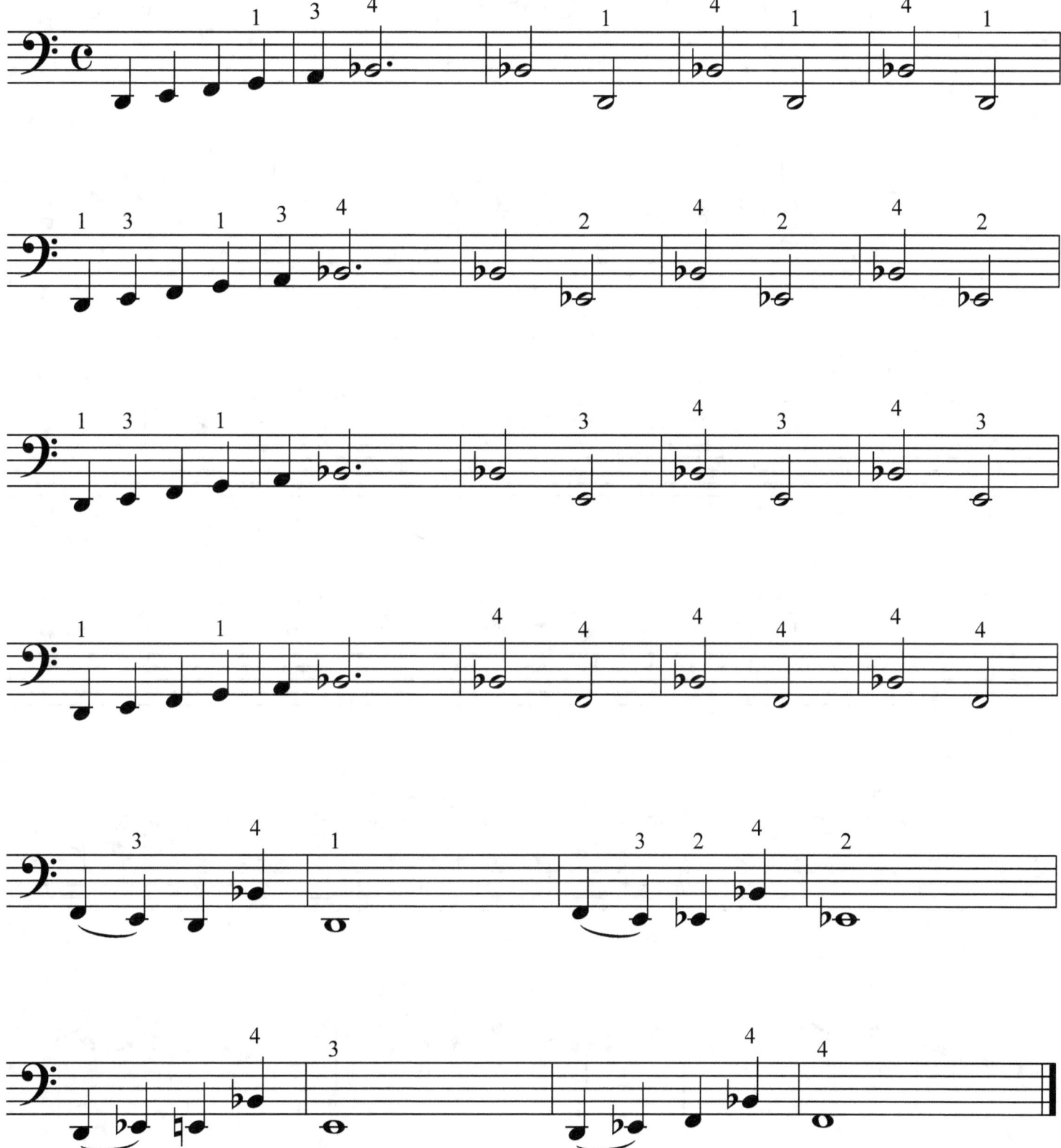

29

Fourth Position Shifting Exercises for the Cello

30

31

Fourth Position Shifting Exercises for the Cello

32

available from **www.charveypublications.com**: CHP332
The Bach Cello Suite No. 1 Study Book

Note: The Suite is broken up into sections in this study book. The complete Suite is at the back of the book.

Suite by J. S. Bach
Exercises by Cassia Harvey

Suite No. 1: Prelude
Part One: Measures 1-4 (Bowing #1)

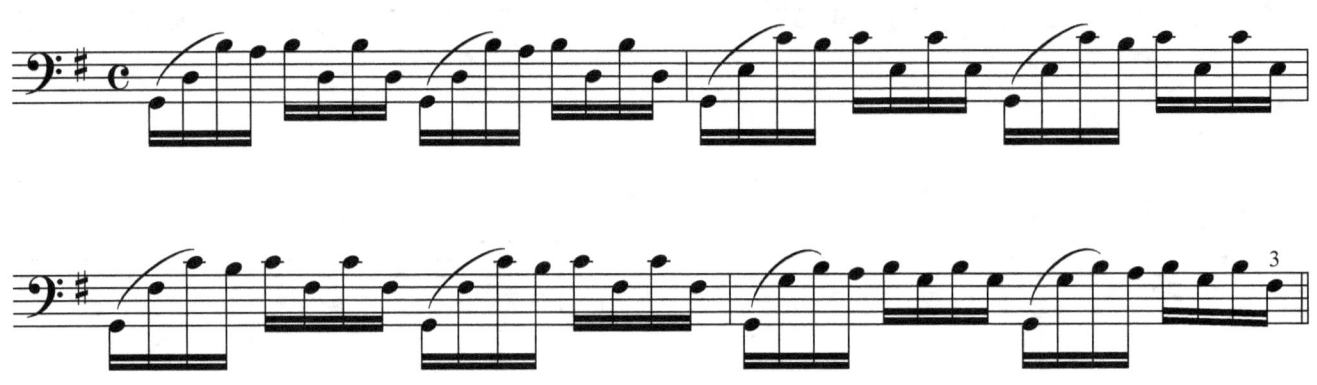

Double Stops for Intonation
Measures 1-4

©2017 C. Harvey Publications All Rights Reserved.

www.ingramcontent.com/pod-product-compliance
Lightning Source LLC
Chambersburg PA
CBHW051428070526
44584CB00023B/3637